HIGHLIGHT REEL

THE TOP PLAYS IN SUPER BOWL HISTORY

BY K. C. KELLEY

SCHOLASTIC INC.

CONTENTS

RETURN OF THE RAVENS!

After the first half of Super Bowl XLVII, the Baltimore Ravens were cruising along. They had outplayed the San Francisco 49ers and held a 21–6 lead. Their defense had picked off the 49ers' Colin Kaepernick and had forced a key fumble. The Niners hoped that half time would give them a chance to get back in the game.

Eleven seconds after the third quarter began, the Niners found themselves in an even deeper hole. Baltimore's Jacoby Jones took the kickoff deep in his own end zone. On most plays like that, the return man will just kneel down. Even the TV commentators were surprised that he started to run it back.

It turned out to be the right choice.

Jones sprinted up the field. He made a sharp cut at about the 10 to elude one Niners tackler. Another bounced off his

FABULOUS FIRSTS!

SUPER BOWL XLVII INCLUDED THE FIRST TIME:

- **THE SUPER BOWL WAS COACHED BY BROTHERS.** Older bro John Harbaugh, coach of the Ravens, beat younger bro Jim Harbaugh, coach of the 49ers.

- **THE SUPER BOWL HAD A BLACKOUT!** Just after the start of the second half (and just after Jones's big play), half of the lights went out in the Superdome! The game was delayed by thirty-four minutes.

- **A FAKE FIELD GOAL WAS ATTEMPTED IN THE GAME'S HISTORY.** Baltimore kicker Justin Tucker was knocked out of bounds one yard short of getting the first down on the second-quarter play.

churning knees a few yards farther on. He found a seam in the coverage, and it was off to the races! Jones sped down the side of the field toward the end zone! One camera angle showed him looking up as he ran. What was he looking at? Himself! Jones watched on the stadium big screen as he ran right into the Super Bowl record book.

Eleven seconds after kickoff, he scored on the longest play in Super Bowl history! Jones's 108-yard return also tied for the second-longest play in NFL history, regular or postseason!

The play's impact on the game was even bigger. The Niners found themselves down by 22 points! No team had ever come back from that many points in a Super Bowl. Jones's play was a backbreaker.

The 49ers did rally, helped by a bizarre power outage. But the Ravens held on at the end to win the game. Without Jones's return, Colin Kaepernick and the Niners

might just have completed their comeback. A daring run by Jones on the game's biggest stage played a huge part in returning the Super Bowl trophy to Baltimore!

LONGEST KICKOFF RETURNS IN SUPER BOWL HISTORY

Yards	Player, Team	Super Bowl
108*	Jacoby Jones, Ravens	XLVII
99	Desmond Howard, Packers	XXXI
98	Fulton Walker, Dolphins	XVII
98	Andre Coleman, Chargers	XXIX
97	Ron Dixon, Giants	XXXV
94	Tim Dwight, Falcons	XXXIII
93	Stanford Jennings, Bengals	XXIII
92	Devin Hester, Bears	XLI

*Also longest play of any kind in Super Bowl history.

RAVENS 34
XLVII
SUPER BOWL
49ERS 31

MARIO'S MAGIC

Super Bowl XLVI was a rematch of the title game played four years earlier: New York Giants vs. New England Patriots. That game ended with an amazing Giants comeback, sparked by a game-changing reception (see page 14).

Guess what? It happened again!

The surprising Giants had won only nine games in the 2012 season. The Patriots were once again heavily favored as the teams met in Indianapolis for the Super Bowl. But a few costly mistakes by the Patriots kept the game close. The Giants trailed by two points when they got the ball back with less than four minutes left in the game. Could Eli Manning lead another comeback drive?

He got them off to the perfect start. From his own 12-yard line, Manning dropped back to pass. He spotted wide receiver Mario Manningham streaking down the left sideline. Manning's high, arcing pass hit Manningham right in the hands at the 46-yard line. At the same instant, Patriots defenders Patrick Chung and Sterling Moore hit Manningham!

Somehow, he managed to get both his feet down, first his right, then his left. As he crashed to the ground out of bounds, he held on to the ball. An official raced in with the signal: It was a catch! New England coach Bill Belichick tossed the red challenge flag on the field, but it didn't matter. Video replay showed Manningham's magic moves in slow motion!

Manningham's tightrope-walking grab sent the Giants racing down the field. Two minutes later, Ahmad Bradshaw strolled untouched into the end zone with the winning touchdown.

Manning and Manningham had teamed up to create yet another incredible pass and catch. A bobble, a slip, one toe on the sideline—anything could have gone wrong. But once again for the Giants and their fans, everything went right.

EXTRA POINT:

This game almost provided another chapter in this book. The Patriots' final Hail Mary pass to end the game just barely escaped the fingers of Rob Gronkowski in the end zone!

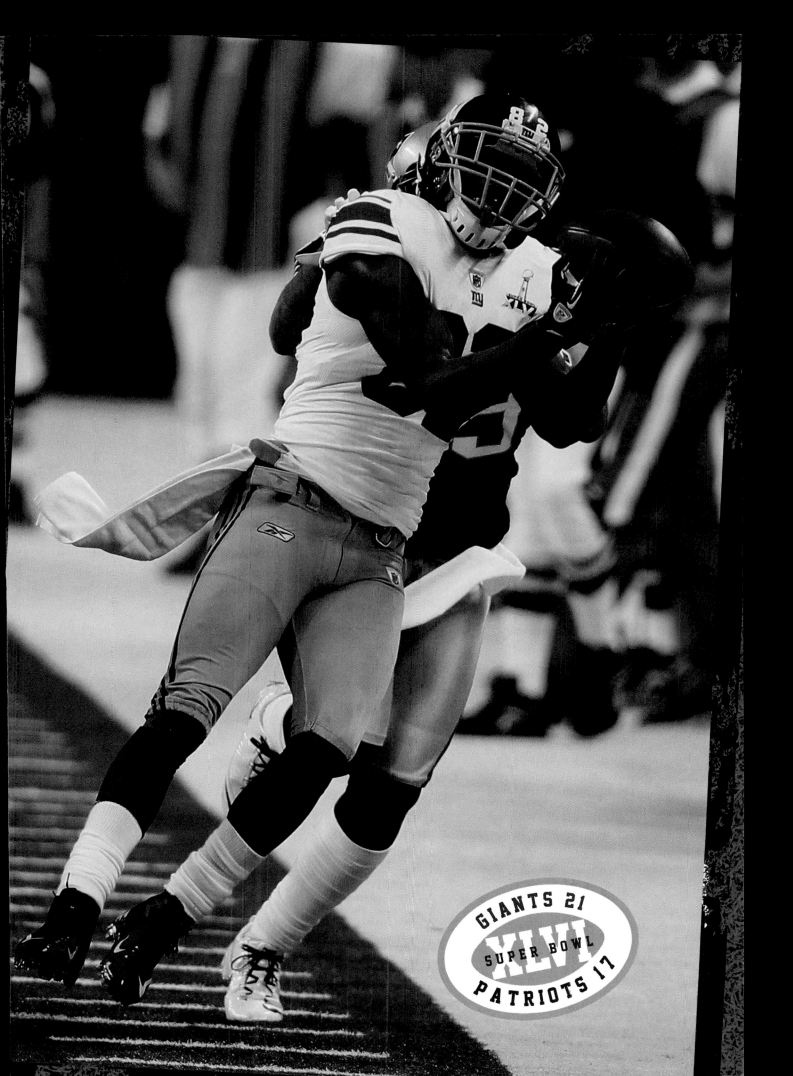

GIANTS 21
XLVI
SUPER BOWL
PATRIOTS 17

SECOND-HALF SURPRISE!

NFL coaches are usually very cautious. A lot is riding on each play, so they usually don't take big chances. Even more is riding on Super Bowl plays, so don't look for a lot of trickery on Super Sunday.

However, because they are so rare, a play like that can be a huge surprise, and if it works, it can turn the game for a team that makes it.

In Super Bowl XLIV, the New Orleans Saints were the underdogs. Peyton Manning and the Indianapolis Colts had dominated the AFC in 2009 and looked unstoppable. The Saints had been superb, too, but most experts gave the edge to the

Colts. In fact, after the first half, the score was closer than people thought it would be, but Indy still led, 10–6.

The Colts would get the ball to start the second half. But New Orleans coach Sean Payton had other ideas. He gathered his team together in the locker room and announced that they would start the second half with "Ambush," their name for an onside kick. It was a stunning move. If it backfired, it might mean the ballgame.

New Orleans went out in its normal kickoff formation. Kicker Thomas Morstead teed the ball up at the 30-yard line. He ran toward the ball as if he was going to boom it downfield. Instead, he

THE ONSIDE KICK RULE

Several rules come into play on onside kick attempts. First, the kicking team has to remain behind the ball until it is kicked, as on all kickoffs. Second, the ball must travel at least 10 yards before it can be recovered by the kicking team. The receiving team can touch it before those 10 yards, however. Once the ball has gone 10 yards or has been touched by the receiving team, it's a live ball. That means either team can recover it.

Since 2009, another rule was added to prevent huge pileups. Before then, a team could put all 10 of its players on one side of the kicker. Now, only five kicking-team players can be on the side the ball is kicked toward.

chipped the ball across his body to the left. It bounced just past the 40 and then back toward the Saints.

Backup defensive back Chris Reis knew what was coming, of course. He sprinted forward and found the ball heading right for him! He hauled it in and pulled it to his chest. Then he waited for the onslaught.

Player after player piled on top of him. Colts and Saints dove in, scrabbling for the ball. Players were pulling and yanking and tugging on one another for more than a minute.

At the bottom of the pile, Reis just held on to the ball for dear life. He said later it felt as if every player on both teams was piled up on top of him! But after everyone was peeled off, the Saints emerged with the football!

The Colts were stunned. The Saints were energized.

The Saints went on to score six plays later and eventually won the game. The surprise worked!

SAINTS 31
XLIV
SUPER BOWL
COLTS 17

HUSTLING HARRISON

In Super Bowl XLIII, the Arizona Cardinals, led by the hard-throwing Kurt Warner, had driven to the Pittsburgh Steelers' 1-yard line. Arizona was behind 10–7 and a touchdown here would give them the lead heading into half time.

With eighteen seconds left, Warner zipped a pass toward Anquan Boldin, who looked open until, out of nowhere, linebacker James Harrison stepped in at the goal line to make the interception. Harrison was supposed to be covering another receiver on the play, but had lost his man. So he just looked for the ball and found it!

As he grabbed the ball and started moving upfield, all he saw was green grass! At nearly 250 pounds, Harrison played to knock people over, not to run. He rumbled up the sideline as the Cardinals began to give chase. Harrison ran with several Steelers who made big blocks.

Inside the 5-yard line, speedy Arizona receiver Larry Fitzgerald finally caught up to Harrison. Could he keep the big man out of the end zone? Fitzgerald, joined by Steve Breaston, hauled Harrison down.

But they were too late. As the trio of players fell, Harrison was in the end zone. A replay official had to double-check, but yes, Harrison had done it. His 100-yard pick-six interception return TD was the longest play in Super Bowl history! (Jacoby Jones later topped that record, but Harrison's is the longest interception return in the big game).

More important for Pittsburgh, it gave them a 17–7 lead instead of looking at a 14–10 deficit.

Harrison had to lie on the ground in the end zone for several minutes to catch his breath. It had been worth it!

But the game wasn't over yet. . . .

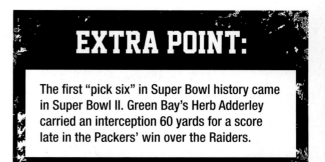

EXTRA POINT:

The first "pick six" in Super Bowl history came in Super Bowl II. Green Bay's Herb Adderley carried an interception 60 yards for a score late in the Packers' win over the Raiders.

TOE-TALLY AWESOME!

With less than a minute to go in Super Bowl XLIII, the Pittsburgh Steelers trailed the surprising Arizona Cardinals by three points. But the Steelers were near the end zone with a chance to win. Big Ben Roethlisberger had moved his team nearly the length of the field in less than three minutes to get into this position. From the 6-yard line, he dropped back and scanned the field as the fans in Tampa's Raymond James Stadium bellowed.

Big Ben saw a flash of white jersey open on the left side of the end zone. This was it! He tossed the ball to Santonio Holmes. The wide receiver jumped for the ball . . . and

missed it! It would have been a great catch had he made it, but he didn't.

So *that* play is not why Holmes is featured in these pages.

"I thought I had lost the Super Bowl," Holmes said later. However, after the miss, there were still forty-two seconds remaining. Pittsburgh had another shot.

The drive to Holmes's big play included overcoming a holding penalty. It also included several key catches by Holmes to help keep the drive alive. The play before his miss, in fact, Holmes had made a 40-yard catch-and-run to set up the team's final shots.

So, on second down, after Holmes's miss, the Steelers tried again. Roethlisberger scrambled to buy time. He evaded one Cardinals tackler. Then he stepped up in the pocket and fired the ball toward the right corner of the end zone. He was aiming at Holmes again, and this time the receiver stretched as far as he could and snagged the ball. Now the trick was to keep his feet inbounds. Like a ballet dancer, he pointed his toes and kicked the red-painted turf. Left, then right, both toes in, and he held the ball!

Touchdown, Steelers—for the win!

STEELERS 27
SUPER BOWL XLIII
CARDINALS 23

HELP FROM A HELMET

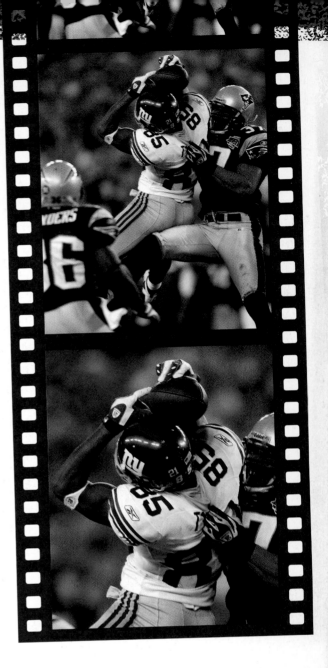

NFL players wear lots of gear to help them do their jobs. Their cleats grip the turf and help them make instant cuts. Their shoulder pads protect them from hard hits. Their gloves help them grip the ball. Their helmets also help them grip the ball.

Wait . . . what?

In Super Bowl XLII, the New York Giants' David Tyree did, in fact, use his helmet to make one of the most spectacular catches in NFL history.

The Giants trailed the New England Patriots late in the fourth quarter. It was third down and five yards to go with just over a minute left. The Giants were on their own 45-yard line, trailing by four. A field goal would not be enough.

Eli Manning went back to pass, but was quickly under attack by rushers. Somehow, he ducked, weaved, and escaped—and then he launched a ball down the middle of the field.

Tyree and New England's Rodney Harrison leaped for the ball at about the 25-yard line. Tyree snagged it and then pressed the ball against his helmet! As he fell to the ground, he somehow managed to hang on, and the ball never hit the ground! The Patriots were stunned, and Giants fans celebrated. Just a few plays later, Manning connected with Plaxico Burress for the game-winning touchdown.

Without Tyree's "sticky" helmet, however, it would have been Patriots Day in Arizona.

GIANTS 17
XLII
SUPER BOWL
PATRIOTS 14

PICK SIX!

Heading into Super Bowl XLI, most fans thought that Peyton Manning would be the man to make the biggest plays. After all, he was the best QB in the NFL and the Indianapolis Colts finally had a chance to win their first Super Bowl.

Manning did make some good plays, including a 53-yard TD pass to Reggie Wayne. But Manning also threw an interception and lost a fumble. The Colts clung to a 22–17 lead in the fourth quarter, but the Bears were driving down the field, hoping for a go-ahead score.

That's when an unlikely hero emerged. Indianapolis cornerback Kelvin Hayden was a rookie in that 2005 season and had not started a single game or picked off any passes. He was in on this Super Bowl play as a nickelback. He found Rex Grossman's pass headed his way and leaped in front of a receiver to make the interception. Next stop, 56 yards later, the end zone for a game-breaking pick six! Hayden's score sealed the win for the Colts and gave Manning his only Super Bowl triumph.

EXTRA POINT:

This game, in Miami, was the first Super Bowl played in the rain.

COLTS 29
XLI
SUPER BOWL
BEARS 17

TWO FOR TWO FOR THREE

Most kickers never get a shot at winning the Super Bowl with a field goal. But Adam Vinatieri got not just one chance, but two! And he made the most of both of them.

The New England Patriots counted on Vinatieri throughout their great Super Bowl run in the early 2000s. His snow-covered boot in the 2001 AFC Championship Game sent New England to their first Super Bowl under coach Bill Belichick.

In that game, Super Bowl XXXVI, the Patriots were outgunned by the mighty St. Louis Rams and outgained by almost 200 yards. However, turnovers and great D had kept the score close. With seven seconds left and the game tied 17–17, the Patriots were at the Rams' 30. And on came Vinatieri. With Super Bowl pressure pounding down, he drilled a 48-yard field goal and the Patriots won their first Super Bowl. It was the first time that a Super Bowl was won on the final play of the game.

Two years later, in Super Bowl XXXVIII, Vinatieri and the Pats got another chance to work their magic. With the scored tied again, this time 29–29 with the Carolina Panthers, quarterback Tom Brady led another drive late in the game. After converting a big third-down play to reach Carolina territory, the Pats reached the 23-yard line with four seconds left.

Once more, the call to Adam. Once more, the kick was good. *Pressure?* thought Vinatieri. *What pressure?*

PATRIOTS 20
SUPER BOWL XXXVI
RAMS 17

PATRIOTS 32
SUPER BOWL XXXVIII
PANTHERS 29

THE TACKLE

Most spectacular game-ending plays come on scores or big kicks. A player reaches the end zone on the final play or a kicker splits the uprights as the clock hits zero.

In Super Bowl XXXIV, however, the game-winning play came thanks to the St. Louis Rams' defense, not from one of its many offense stars.

The high-scoring Rams led 23–16 late in the game, but the Tennessee Titans were giving St. Louis all it could handle. Titans QB Steve McNair didn't have the firepower of the Rams' Kurt Warner, but he was proving to be a big-game leader. He marched the Titans toward the end zone as time ran down.

McNair hit Kevin Dyson with a pass to the Rams' 10-yard line. The Titans had no time-outs, so they quickly ran another play. Since the Rams would expect a play to the end zone, McNair tried to sneak a pass underneath to Dyson so he could run it in. But linebacker Mike Jones saw through the trick. He ran up to grab Dyson around the legs. Though the wide receiver stretched all he could, Jones held Dyson just inches short of the score as time ran out.

"The Tackle" now lives on in Super Bowl history.

RAMS 23
SUPER BOWL
XXXIV
TITANS 16

HELICOPTER JOHN

John Elway of the Denver Broncos had come so close so often. He had lost three Super Bowls and nearly made it to several others. Now, in Super Bowl XXXII, against the Green Bay Packers, they had another shot. The score was tied at 17–17 late in the third quarter. That's when Elway and his thirty-seven-year-old body came through with one of the most famous runs in the game's history.

From the Packers' 12-yard line, he dropped back to pass. But the Green Bay rush flushed him from the pocket. Elway scrambled and found a path toward the end zone. He took a quick glance at the sideline . . . he knew how much he needed for the first down. As he crossed the 5-yard line, two Packers neared him. Elway dove headfirst and was hit in midair. His body spun around like helicopter blades. As he fell to the ground, he had a key Broncos

first down. He popped up, pumped his fist, and then led Denver to a go-ahead score by Terrell Davis. The hit energized and inspired the Broncos and they went on to win, finally.

The Broncos and their Hall of Fame quarterback finally had their Super Bowl rings.

BRONCOS 31
SUPER BOWL XXXII
PACKERS 24

PICTURE PERFECT

The Green Bay Packers were leading Super Bowl XXXI in the third quarter. But their margin over the New England Patriots was only six points, and the Patriots had just scored to make it that close. The Packers needed a big play to get their momentum back.

Time for Desmond Howard to do his thing.

Everyone knew Howard's skill at returning punts. He had led the NFL that season (1996) with three punt-return scores and 875 return yards. He had also returned 22 kickoffs, but he hadn't taken one of those to the house.

As a packed Superdome crowd roared, Howard took the Patriots kickoff and headed upfield. He passed through the first crowd of tacklers, then broke away from one Patriot at about the 30. Then it was a race, and he wasn't going to lose it.

Howard said later he had some help on his record 99-yard TD. As he neared the end zone, he looked up at the giant video screen to watch himself. He could see that no one was chasing him, so he watched himself score the big TD on TV!

Howard became the only special-teams player named Super Bowl MVP.

EXTRA POINT:

Howard's 99-yard play was the longest in Super Bowl history until James Harrison's 100-yard play (see page 10).

PACKERS 35
SUPER BOWL XXXI
PATRIOTS 21

BEEBE'S BEST

Things we learned from watching Leon Lett and Don Beebe in Super Bowl XXVII:

- Don Beebe was wicked fast.
- Defensive linemen do not score often.
- Don't celebrate too early!

Those lessons came after a memorable play in 1993. Lett's Dallas Cowboys were demolishing Beebe's Buffalo Bills. It ended up being one of the biggest blowouts in Super Bowl history. But it could have been worse if not for Beebe.

With just under five minutes left, the Cowboys forced a Bills fumble. Lett picked up the ball at the Cowboys' 36-yard line and headed for the end zone. Beebe, a wide receiver, was far downfield—the other way—on a pass pattern. As Lett began rumbling for six, Beebe sprinted almost the length of the field. He ran 90 yards to Lett's 64.

A few steps before he reached the promised land, Lett held the ball out to his side to celebrate. Beebe reached him just before the goal line and swatted the ball away. Lett collapsed in the end zone in shock. And coaches everywhere got a lesson on "never give up."

Beebe later told Lett that he was just going to jump on his back until he held out the ball. For his part, Lett took it with good humor. After all, he had a Super Bowl ring—and he made sure not to fumble that!

EXTRA POINT:

There was no instant replay in the NFL for this game. The officials had to make the call right away based on what they saw.

COWBOYS 52
SUPER BOWL XXVII
BILLS 17

Scott Norwood of the Buffalo Bills was three for four on kicks in Super Bowl XXV, making a field goal and a pair of extra points. Usually, that would be a pretty good day. But since his one miss came on the final play of the game, it was anything but.

The Bills came into Super Bowl XXV with one of the NFL's highest-scoring offenses. But the New York Giants used a game plan designed to keep the Bills' offense off the field. The score was close all the way through. Early in the fourth quarter, in fact, the Bills pulled ahead 19–17. A few minutes later, the Giants retook the lead on a Matt Bahr field goal.

As the clock wound down, the Bills got one more chance to take the lead. Quarterback Jim Kelly, however, could only get the ball to the Giants' 30-yard line. There was time for just one more play. Norwood lined up for a 47-yard field goal attempt that would give Buffalo the win. It was a pretty long kick. And while Norwood had led the NFL with 52 PATs (point after touchdown) in the 1990 season, he had made only 69 percent of his field goal attempts.

And he missed this one, too. His kick sailed to the right of the uprights.

The Bills' anguish was as big as the Giants' joy.

GIANTS 20
SUPER BOWL XXV
BILLS 19

EXTRA POINT:

The Giants kept the powerful Bills' offense off the field by controlling the ball. They set a record for possession: 40 minutes, 33 seconds.

A STUPENDOUS SECOND

In Super Bowl XXII, the Washington Redskins fell behind the Denver Broncos 10–0 in the first quarter. It didn't look good for quarterback Doug Williams.

Then the second quarter started . . . and the game was quickly over.

In that record-setting period, Williams threw four touchdown passes on the way to Washington scoring five times. The 35-point outburst is still the most ever in the postseason in one quarter.

The scoring binge began with an 80-yard catch-and-run to Ricky Sanders. A few minutes later, Williams hit Gary Clark at the goal line with a 27-yard toss for score number two. After a 58-yard run by Timmy Smith, Williams struck again. He arced a long, high pass to Sanders, who ran the final yards into the end zone. Washington and Williams wrapped up their stunning second quarter with an 8-yard TD pass to tight end Clint Didier.

Amazingly, that whole string of scoring took just eighteen plays while using up less than six minutes on the scoreboard clock.

Williams was named MVP of the Redskins' 42–10 triumph, setting then–Super Bowl records with 340 passing yards and those four TD passes.

EXTRA POINT:

Doug Williams was the first African American to start at quarterback in a Super Bowl.

REDSKINS 42
SUPER BOWL
XXII
BRONCOS 10

MONTANA MAGIC

Joe Montana and the San Francisco 49ers had three minutes to go and 92 yards to score. They trailed the Cincinnati Bengals 16–13 in Super Bowl XXIII. A field goal would tie the game, but a touchdown would clinch the win.

With his usual cool style, Montana mixed runs and short passes, including several to MVP Jerry Rice, to steer the Niners to the Bengals' 10-yard line with thirty-nine seconds left. He called the play: 20 Halfback Curl X Up. Rice would be a decoy, while running back Roger Craig was a safety valve to the outside. The main target would be John Taylor, slanting in from the left.

The tricky part was that Montana had just a tiny window to get the ball to Taylor. Any slipup would mean disaster. At the snap, Taylor faked left, then slanted right. Montana took a short drop and fired! Bang! Right into Taylor's hands! The Niners had done it: a last-minute, field-spanning, Super Bowl–winning drive!

Believe it or not, Taylor only made one catch during the game—the biggest one.

EXTRA POINT:

The 49ers became the first team from the NFC to win three Super Bowls. Two AFC teams, the Raiders and Steelers, also had that many at this point.

49ERS 20
SUPER BOWL
XXIII
BENGALS 16

THE FRIDGE!

William Perry was the first, largest, and only household appliance to score in a Super Bowl game. Perry's nickname was "the Refrigerator," or simply . . . "the Fridge." And if you ever saw his massive frame, you'd understand why. He weighed well over 300 pounds and usually played defensive tackle for the mighty Chicago Bears.

But once in a while, Bears coach Mike Ditka put the football in Fridge's hands and dared anyone to try to tackle him.

In Super Bowl XX, Fridge got his chance to put the freeze on the New England Patriots. Late in the third quarter, the Bears were running away with the game. They led 37–3 when they reached the Patriots' 1-yard line. To the delight of fans at the Superdome and watching on TV, Perry set up behind the quarterback for the goal-line play. He took the handoff, followed a blocker, and crashed into the end zone. Perry hauled himself to his feet and nearly popped the football with a massive spike for an all-time Super Bowl highlight.

EXTRA POINT:

The Fridge was part of a Chicago defense that only allowed 7 rushing yards to the Patriots—a Super Bowl record.

BEARS 46
SUPER BOWL XX
PATRIOTS 10

ALLEN'S AMAZING!

Players who were on the field still remember it as one of the best plays they were ever part of. Fans who were there aren't sure what they saw. Even fans who watch the video can't believe it. On the final play of the third quarter of Super Bowl XVIII, Marcus Allen of the Los Angeles Raiders made a run that, well, we're still talking about it now, almost thirty years later.

The play started as a simple sweep left. The Raiders' guard and tackle pulled that way. Allen took the handoff and started to follow. But the Washington Redskins' right linebacker covered the outside and Allen had nowhere to go except back the way he came.

Stutter-stepping, he spun around and ran back toward the center of the field. As he ran along the line of scrimmage, he spotted an opening. As Redskins bounced off him, he blew threw the hole. He was almost in the clear. At the 50-yard line, he sprinted past two more players. Then it was a race to the end zone, and Allen won.

His back and forth, game-busting, 74-yard run put the game out of reach, 34–9. The two teams played the fourth quarter, but it hardly mattered. The Raiders had clinched the Super Bowl title as soon as Allen sprinted into the end zone.

RAIDERS 38
XVIII
SUPER BOWL
REDSKINS 9

RIGGINS'S RUMBLE

The Washington Redskins trailed the Miami Dolphins 17–13 in the fourth quarter of Super Bowl XVII. The Skins needed about a foot for a first down just past midfield. They had to go for it to try to keep their drive going. If they failed, Miami might be able to go the other way for a game-clinching score. But running back John Riggins was not satisfied with just a foot. He wanted the whole thing.

Washington ran a play called 70 Chip. Clint Didier started in front of Riggins and blocked a Miami safety. That left big "Riggo" alone against Don McNeal. It was an uneven match. McNeal got a hold of Riggins's jersey, but the big running back just shook McNeal off with one shove. After that it was a race, and Riggins won. He scored a 43-yard touchdown that gave

EXTRA POINT:

The great blocking on this big play came from Washington's offensive line. Their famous nickname? The Hogs.

Washington the lead for good. At the time, it was the longest touchdown run in Super Bowl history.

Quarterback Joe Theismann later summed up what the Redskins thought going into the big play: *We're bigger, we're badder, we're better than you are. Now stop us.* The Dolphins couldn't, and the Redskins were champs.

REDSKINS 27
SUPER BOWL XVII
DOLPHINS 17

NONE SHALL PASS!

For most of the first three quarters of Super Bowl XVI, the San Francisco 49ers were in charge over the Cincinnati Bengals. San Francisco led 20–7, but Cincinnati was on a roll. Their offense started clicking and suddenly, they were on the San Francisco 3-yard line. A score would inch them closer and swing momentum their way for the important final quarter.

The two teams towered over the ball, hundreds of pounds of people on either side.

First down: Pete Johnson slammed into the line, but 49ers linebacker Jack Reynolds met him head on. No score.

Second down: Johnson again, and this time it was John Harty who made the hit.

Third down: The Bengals tried a short pass. Linebacker Dan Bunz smacked into receiver Charles Alexander and stood him up. All Alexander had to do was fall forward and he would have scored. Bunz stopped him.

Fourth down: The Bengals tried Johnson again. This time, the entire Niners line rose up and stopped him. Bunz later said he hit the runner so hard that screws in his facemask came loose!

After the game, coach Bill Walsh called the fourth-down stop "the play that won the game for us."

The Niners added another score and held on to win their first Super Bowl, thanks to a mighty goal-line stand.

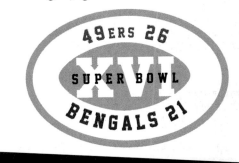

EXTRA POINT:

Many of the Niners nearly missed the kickoff! One of the buses bringing the team to the game got caught in traffic!

SWANN DIVE

NFL teams didn't always pass as often as they do today. In Super Bowl X, for example, Pittsburgh threw only nineteen times. Fortunately, the Steelers' Lynn Swann caught four of those passes. One of them was among the most memorable in Super Bowl history.

In the second quarter, Pittsburgh was trapped deep in Dallas Cowboys territory. QB Terry Bradshaw launched a bomb in Swann's direction. Just at midfield, Swann and Dallas DB Mark Washington leaped for the ball. Swann tipped it and then was knocked forward by Washington. Both men fell, and the ball floated along with them. Swann calmly tipped the ball in the air, and as he landed on his back, the ball landed on his chest and he gathered it in. Amazing!

Later in the game, Swann scored what would prove to the game winner. Swann hauled in a 64-yard touchdown pass from Bradshaw to give Pittsburgh its final points. For helping Pittsburgh climb out of a hole and then clinch the win, Swann was named the game's MVP.

REDSKINS 27
SUPER BOWL
XVII
DOLPHINS 17

EXTRA POINT:

Swann set a Super Bowl record with 161 receiving yards. The current record is 215 yards by Jerry Rice of San Francisco in Super Bowl XXIII.

GARO'S GOOF

Garo Yepremian played kicker in the NFL for fourteen seasons. In six of those seasons, he didn't miss a single extra point. He also led the league three times in field-goal percentage. But after all that, everyone remembers just one play: the time he tried to pass.

In Super Bowl VII, the Miami Dolphins were cruising. Their powerful defense had kept the Washington Redskins from scoring at all. By late in the fourth quarter, Miami led 14–0. With just over two minutes left, the Dolphins lined up for Yepremian to try a field goal to ice the game. It didn't quite work out.

Yepremian's low kick was blocked. It bounced back toward him. Instead of just running away from it, he picked it up! The tiny kicker rolled out, looking to throw the ball to a teammate. That didn't work out, either. The ball flopped out of his hands

EXTRA POINT:

The victory made the Dolphins 17–0 for the entire season. They are still the only NFL team to finish undefeated during the Super Bowl era.

like a lost butterfly. Washington's Mike Bass snatched it out of the air and ran 49 yards for a touchdown. As Miami held on to the lead for the final two minutes, Yepremian was the most nervous guy in the stadium. But the Dolphins won anyway, and Yepremian still laughs about the event today, proud of his Super Bowl ring.

DOLPHINS 14
SUPER BOWL VII
REDSKINS 7

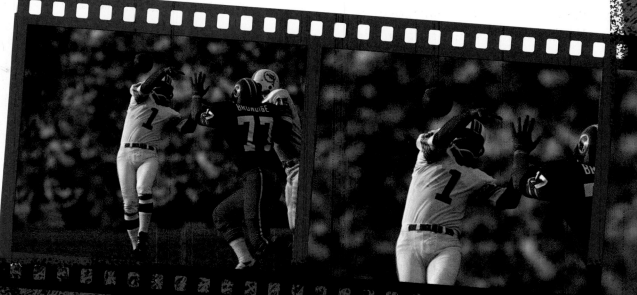

THE KID COMES THROUGH

The Baltimore Colts teased their young kicker, Jim O'Brien, about his long hair. It was 1971 and football players didn't generally let their hair grow. O'Brien didn't mind. He was a pretty easygoing guy who loved to kick footballs—and catch them, too. He was also a wide receiver for Baltimore.

But when it came time to kick a game-winning field goal in Super Bowl V, against the Indianapolis Colts, O'Brien wasn't quite as easygoing. How nervous was O'Brien? As was his habit, he tried to pluck some grass from the field so he could toss it in the air to judge the wind direction. One problem: The game was played on artificial turf!

But O'Brien shoved his nerves aside, took two big steps, and slammed the ball 32 yards, right through the uprights. (He kicked it with his toe in the straight-ahead style of the day.) The young kicker leaped for joy as his teammates crowded around him. It didn't matter then how long his hair was, just how long the kick had been!

The Colts had to survive the ensuing kickoff, but after they did, the game ended. It was the first time that a Super Bowl had come down to a game-deciding kick, but it wouldn't be the last!

COLTS 16
SUPER BOWL V
COWBOYS 13

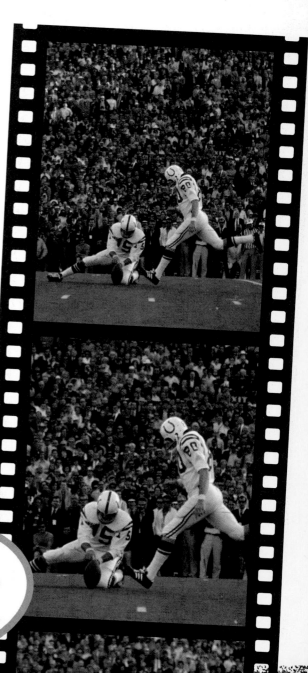

SUPER MAX!

Max McGee caught four passes for the Green Bay Packers during the 1966 NFL season. He was basically a backup, rarely seeing action in games. But when the Packers won the NFL Championship and earned a spot, against the Kansas City Chiefs, in the first Super Bowl, McGee took center stage.

Starting receiver Boyd Dowler was injured early in the game. Coach Vince Lombardi called on the veteran backup—and a star was born. About nine minutes into the game, McGee caught a 37-yard pass from Bart Starr to score the first touchdown in Super Bowl history. The surprise star ended up with seven catches for 138 yards, both of which were more than he had had that entire season! He even added a second score in the third quarter for good measure. When the game began, most fans thought Starr or running back Jim Taylor would be the Packers' heroes. No one expected it to be McGee . . . least of all Max himself!

PACKERS 35
SUPER BOWL I
CHIEFS 10

EXTRA POINT:

In his first six NFL seasons, McGee doubled as the Packers' punter!

ALL-TIME SUPER BOWL RESULTS

Game	Date	Winning team	Score	Losing team	MVP	Position
I	January 15, 1967	Green Bay Packers	35–10	Kansas City Chiefs	Bart Starr	Quarterback
II	January 14, 1968	Green Bay Packers	33–14	Oakland Raiders	Bart Starr	Quarterback
III	January 12, 1969	New York Jets	16–7	Baltimore Colts	Joe Namath	Quarterback
IV	January 11, 1970	Kansas City Chiefs	23–7	Minnesota Vikings	Len Dawson	Quarterback
V	January 17, 1971	Baltimore Colts	16–13	Dallas Cowboys	Chuck Howley	Linebacker
VI	January 16, 1972	Dallas Cowboys	24–3	Miami Dolphins	Roger Staubach	Quarterback
VII	January 14, 1973	Miami Dolphins	14–7	Washington Redskins	Jake Scott	Safety
VIII	January 13, 1974	Miami Dolphins	24–7	Minnesota Vikings	Larry Csonka	Running back
IX	January 12, 1975	Pittsburgh Steelers	16–6	Minnesota Vikings	Franco Harris	Running back
X	January 18, 1976	Pittsburgh Steelers	21–17	Dallas Cowboys	Lynn Swann	Wide receiver
XI	January 9, 1977	Oakland Raiders	32–14	Minnesota Vikings	Fred Biletnikoff	Wide receiver
XII	January 15, 1978	Dallas Cowboys	27–10	Denver Broncos	Harvey Martin Randy White	Defensive end Defensive tackle
XIII	January 21, 1979	Pittsburgh Steelers	35–31	Dallas Cowboys	Terry Bradshaw	Quarterback
XIV	January 20, 1980	Pittsburgh Steelers	31–19	Los Angeles Rams	Terry Bradshaw	Quarterback
XV	January 25, 1981	Oakland Raiders	27–10	Philadelphia Eagles	Jim Plunkett	Quarterback
XVI	January 24, 1982	San Francisco 49ers	26–21	Cincinnati Bengals	Joe Montana	Quarterback
XVII	January 30, 1983	Washington Redskins	27–17	Miami Dolphins	John Riggins	Running back
XVIII	January 22, 1984	Los Angeles Raiders	38–9	Washington Redskins	Marcus Allen	Running back
XIX	January 20, 1985	San Francisco 49ers	38–16	Miami Dolphins	Joe Montana	Quarterback
XX	January 26, 1986	Chicago Bears	46–10	New England Patriots	Richard Dent	Defensive end
XXI	January 25, 1987	New York Giants	39–20	Denver Broncos	Phil Simms	Quarterback
XXII	January 31, 1988	Washington Redskins	42–10	Denver Broncos	Doug Williams	Quarterback
XXIII	January 22, 1989	San Francisco 49ers	20–16	Cincinnati Bengals	Jerry Rice	Wide receiver
XXIV	January 28, 1990	San Francisco 49ers	55–10	Denver Broncos	Joe Montana	Quarterback
XXV	January 27, 1991	New York Giants	20–19	Buffalo Bills	Ottis Anderson	Running back
XXVI	January 26, 1992	Washington Redskins	37–24	Buffalo Bills	Mark Rypien	Quarterback
XXVII	January 31, 1993	Dallas Cowboys	52–17	Buffalo Bills	Troy Aikman	Quarterback
XXVIII	January 30, 1994	Dallas Cowboys	30–13	Buffalo Bills	Emmitt Smith	Running back
XXIX	January 29, 1995	San Francisco 49ers	49–26	San Diego Chargers	Steve Young	Quarterback
XXX	January 28, 1996	Dallas Cowboys	27–17	Pittsburgh Steelers	Larry Brown	Cornerback
XXXI	January 26, 1997	Green Bay Packers	35–21	New England Patriots	Desmond Howard	Kickoff/punt returner
XXXII	January 25, 1998	Denver Broncos	31–24	Green Bay Packers	Terrell Davis	Running back
XXXIII	January 31, 1999	Denver Broncos	34–19	Atlanta Falcons	John Elway	Quarterback
XXXIV	January 30, 2000	St. Louis Rams	23–16	Tennessee Titans	Kurt Warner	Quarterback
XXXV	January 28, 2001	Baltimore Ravens	34–7	New York Giants	Ray Lewis	Linebacker
XXXVI	February 3, 2002	New England Patriots	20–17	St. Louis Rams	Tom Brady	Quarterback
XXXVII	January 26, 2003	Tampa Bay Buccaneers	48–21	Oakland Raiders	Dexter Jackson	Safety
XXXVIII	February 1, 2004	New England Patriots	32–29	Carolina Panthers	Tom Brady	Quarterback
XXXIX	February 6, 2005	New England Patriots	24–21	Philadelphia Eagles	Deion Branch	Wide receiver
XL	February 5, 2006	Pittsburgh Steelers	21–10	Seattle Seahawks	Hines Ward	Wide receiver
XLI	February 4, 2007	Indianapolis Colts	29–17	Chicago Bears	Peyton Manning	Quarterback
XLII	February 3, 2008	New York Giants	17–14	New England Patriots	Eli Manning	Quarterback
XLIII	February 1, 2009	Pittsburgh Steelers	27–23	Arizona Cardinals	Santonio Holmes	Wide receiver
XLIV	February 7, 2010	New Orleans Saints	31–17	Indianapolis Colts	Drew Brees	Quarterback
XLV	February 6, 2011	Green Bay Packers	31–25	Pittsburgh Steelers	Aaron Rodgers	Quarterback
XLVI	February 5, 2012	New York Giants	21–17	New England Patriots	Eli Manning	Quarterback
XLVII	February 3, 2013	Baltimore Ravens	34–31	San Francisco 49ers	Joe Flacco	Quarterback